ten degrees each:

thirty-six poems for life

Ten Degrees Each: Thirty-Six Poems for Life
Copyright © 2021, Janice Ballard

Park Point Press
573 Park Point Drive
Golden, CO 80401-7402
720-496-1370

www.csl.org/publications/books
www.scienceofmind.com/publish-your-book

Printed in the United States of America
Published September 2021

Editor: Julie Mierau, JM Wordsmith
Design/Layout: Maria Robinson, Designs On You, LLC

ISBN paperback: 978-0-917849-98-5
ISBN ebook: 978-0-917849-99-2

"God is a circle

whose center is everywhere and

circumference nowhere."

~Voltaire

ten degrees each:

thirty-six poems for life

janice ballard

Park Point
PRESS

Park Point Press is an imprint of Centers for Spiritual Living
573 Park Point Drive | Golden CO 80401

introduction

These poems found their way to the page during the COVID-19 pandemic of 2020-2021.

It all started with the poem "Pandemic Birdsong," and it happened just as I describe in my poem, "Word by Word."

I once read of a poet who said she had to "run like hell" from her daily walk in the woods to capture a poem that was passing through her. She described it as a feeling that the poem was rushing right through her body. These poems came to me in much the same way. They were written before I knew it, and I was merely the scribe.

This has been a time of transformation for many and most certainly for me. If I listened well during this time to the still small voice within and captured the messages on these pages, you might be able hear words of inspiration and elevation, truth and praise for the amazing and limitless world we are privileged to be living in.

I want to thank the members of my writing group, who suggested the title for this collection. When I told them I had thirty-six poems to share in this book, they immediately responded with the idea of *Ten Degrees Each,* and *Thirty-Six Poems For Life* seemed the likely subtitle. The idea resonated with my deep affinity for circles—symbols of vitality, wholeness, completion, and perfection.

I offer these poems to you, dear reader, that they may encircle you with a profound sense of Spirit.

table of contents

ten degrees

each:

thirty-six poems

for life

pandemic birdsong

Do you think the birds know why we stay inside?
Do they notice that we walk, not drive,
we meander, not rush,
we stop to talk to our neighbors for a longer time,
maintaining our six-foot distance?
Do the birds look in our windows and
wonder why we sit and talk to each other more,
working on puzzles and making art,
creating dance parties and online celebrations,
cooking thoughtful meals and lingering at the table
longer with no place to go but
deeper into ourselves and our homes?
Do the birds know that we listen to their
pleasing songs with renewed interest or
new interest, marveling over and over again
at the sweet melodies that hardly caught our
attention before?
Do they see us watching them feed
their babies in their carefully crafted
and organic nests, remembering our own
childhood or parenthood,
hearing us pledge to stay in this conscious
and deliberate way of living life fully, with
attention and intention?

Live more fully, she said,
audacious, dynamic light bearers that you are
and always have been.
The time is now,
the day is here, the moment
has arrived, your transformation
stands boldly before you,
beckoning you to open doors and
windows long shuttered and bolted
by doubts and fears.
Ride on the waves that take us out to sea,
and know that you
are one with every drop in the ocean,
every molecule of sky and air,
each current of wind that encircles you with
the spirit of truth and wisdom.
Fear does not live in these
environs, this domain of reality
calling us.
A union that cannot be divided,
a purpose unlimited and
infinite.

Recognize the need to survive,
seek remedies,
make plans,
awaken and fill the day
with necessary actions.
Following the edges of the square,
walking and running along the
straight lines.
Embrace the need to thrive,
making spaces
with expressions of
deep nourishment,
food for the soul,
breathing in and soaring
around concentric circles,
moving in and out and back again,
a burgeoning and creative
wellspring renewing itself with
action and inaction,
building moments of passion and union,
relating to self and others, words and stories,
pigments and paintings.
Squares and circles intersecting,
surviving and thriving through
this new life,
moving in and out to the rhythm of our breath.

faith is a verb

"I am faithing," I said,
waving my faith wand
at the circumstances
and events around me.
How else will I find my oneness?
How else will I transform the world?
The injustice, the abominations, the wounded and
forsaken deserve my unwavering commitment.
If I don't believe, find faith, how will I go on?
How will I go on?
I have limped along, sat immobile, receding into the shadows,
failing to question, confront, risk or make demands for change.
It's time for change, I cry out,
It's time for radical change, I write,
It's time for equality and transformation, I sing.
It's time my heart opens to and remains wide open
to the feelings and actions that deserve my
wholehearted conviction.
Let me be unwavering, willing and able,
an instrument for all that is good.

for one and for all

The need for change
cries out from the
depths of our soul.
The oversoul of our country
calls us to search inside,
to transform the outside.
It calls on us to
seek ways to change hearts,
form minds, act with justice,
create peace.
The time is now,
to journey deep for answers,
to break down walls and systems,
to each be the uprising that births
and cultivates, nurtures and
fosters new systems for
being members of this
life we share.
How did we get so far away
from Truth?
Seek to know,
then move from dark toward
light to live the Truth that
calls us to oneness,
calls us to equality,
calls us to bring light, be light
to the world.

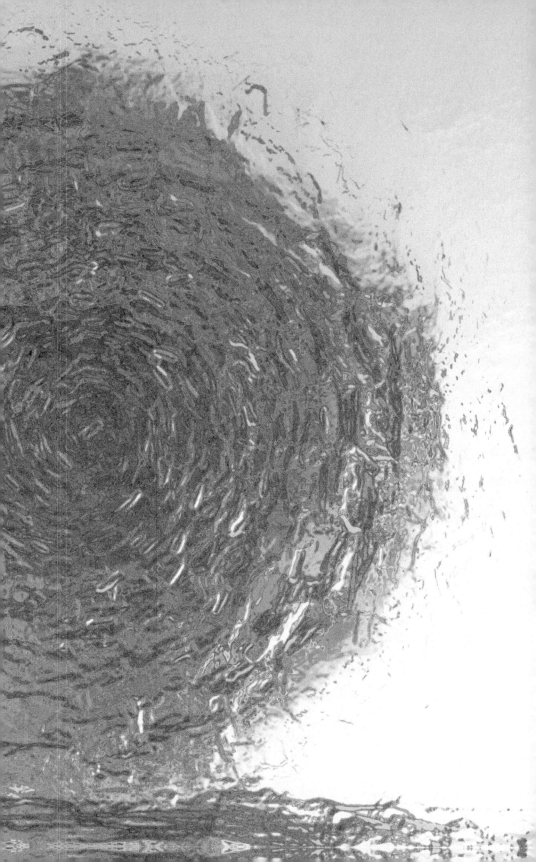

not just another love poem

It has likely all been said,
words and phrases
extolling the desire for it,
advice to cherish it,
warnings to not reject it.
proposals on how to live and
die for it,
romantic, playful, enduring,
obsessive, agape,
thousands of years attempting to
define and praise its virtues.
But that's just not enough for me right now —

I want to become it, love.
Full-fledged, driving force, breaking open,
weathering every kind of storm, love.
The sustaining, penetrating and powerful,
omnipotent and omnipresent, love.

Free of all armor,
I want to be clothed in It,
flowing and breathing,
sheer fabric spun with
leaves stirring on the gentle breeze,

adorned with playful shadows,
luminescent in the silent light of
each sunrise and sunset.
Mastering it, vibrating with it
at the deepest level.

not just another love poem

I turned myself inside out

"I turned outside in," I told her.
"No," said the sage,
"you turned yourself
inside out."

"You are looking for the key," she offered.
It resonated and I continued the search,
knowing I was looking to open up.
The key was buried, not the treasure.
It was out in the open,
an enormous matter of fact and
truth.

"I will study," I proclaimed.
"Look inside," I was directed.
Then out and in became blurred
and clear at the same time.
No difference between every
living thing and the being that
sourced this wonder.

"Can I be a poet?" I asked.
"You are." I heard.
So I wrote the words

as I heard them,
playing the keys like a piano.
Wanting to share the tempo
And the melody, finding
a different music for the ear.

I turned myself inside out

She has from the moment of her conception, through
the moments of each of our conceptions, nurtured us.
Our genetic code, a helix of perfect union
with each and every atom
and element, made us One.
Giver of all life, gifting us with
opulent sunrises, meticulous formations of migrating birds,
curling waves hitting the shore,
stone forests carved from the rocks and
strata of eons.
Mountains reaching up to give
homage to the clouds,
as revolving colors of azure blue and fiery
red, majestic purples, and the whole spectrum and
mixture of imaginable colors and non-colors change
before our eyes.

She built a home for every creature, great and small,
fed us from her richness,
breath in our lungs, and the warmth of her stars.
The Earth gave us
her melodies of wind,
her textures of sharp and smooth,
The scent of warm pine needles and lilacs and olive trees.
The Earth gave the seen and unseen to us,

the roaring of the waves and stillness of early morning,
presenting each pure silence so our senses could feel
more deeply her infinite cycles.
Always with a humble heart, never asking from us.
Let us not turn a blind eye to demise,
to the Earth's despair and the cry of the creatures.
Open wide to the gratitude and respect growing
inside of us, the power to be.
As within, so without, healing of self,
healing the wholeness of this world.
The Earth and I are One,
bred from the same Mother, Father, Spirit.

spirit of the earth

damn those boots!

I kicked them, I tripped over them,
I moved them only
to move them back to their
perilous perch by the front door.
I avoided getting their message about change,
and they continued to call out to me their warning.
It's the simple things,
 the low-hanging branches that swipe my face
or the puzzle boxes that tumble out of the closet each time it's opened.
It's the wishing year after year that a relationship would be different,
a job more fulfilling, that a depression will lift and I will be anew.
Is it insanity that propels us to do the same thing over and over again
expecting different results or is it our comfort with the routine,
the predictable unpredictability?
With perseverance, the frustrating catalyst
can shove me so hard I hit the wall and
I must decide if I will shuffle my feet trying
to move the mountain of a wall for hours or weeks or years or
simply change direction, reorient myself
to the world today, now.
We are new each moment, malleable, flexible.
I can change direction, I can change, I can!

The choice to move one degree or 359 degrees can yield
amazing, transforming, vibrant waves of

life's possibilities that dance around me offering resilience,
and an irrepressible freedom to leap into the unknown.

Watch what I trip over, bang my head on and then,
like a moth attracted to light, orient myself to
the boundless regions of life inviting me to hold on and
take the ride.

damn those boots!

prayer flags

They whisper their intentions,
perpetually responding to the breeze,
an inspired ebb and flow of holy words
and works, an undulating motion that calls forth
the peace, the healing,
the abundance consecrated in the
patterns of red, green, yellow, white.

A mantra riding on the wind, higher and higher,
traveling miles and miles away,
resonating with all the prayers
offered in quiet temples of smoky incense
and candlelight, devotion,
aspiration and inspiration.

These colorful rectangles, moving reminders,
invoking enlightenment and compassion.
Rise up — fill the sky with the deep desires for
all humanity.
Spiritual beings seeking sacred matters.

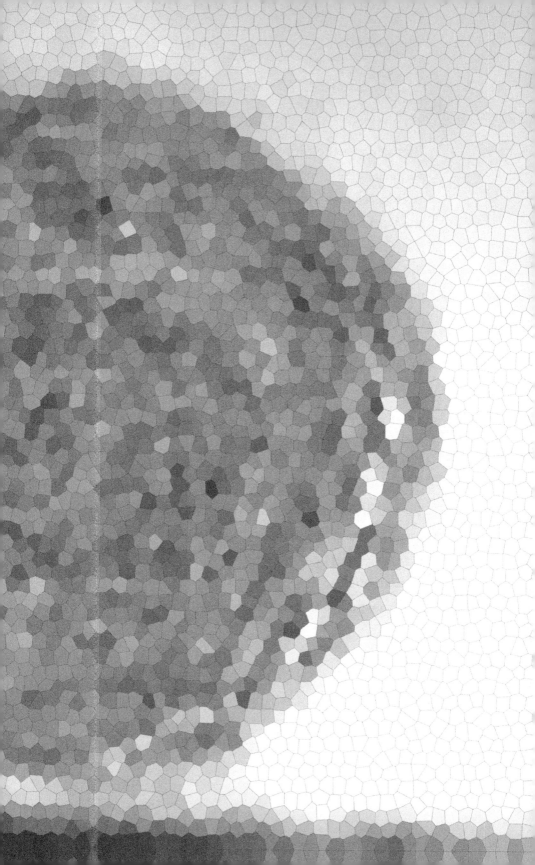

The eyes truly are the windows to the soul —
he spoke these words ever sure of the power of
outer signs of inner states of mind and being.
A portrait of our innermost selves.
Painting the shapes and colors of
deep love and compassion,
tremulous fear, nagging doubt.
Eyes shining with eagerness and quiet,
faithful surrender to stories that offer change and hope.
Eyes reflecting openness and receptivity to
risk and adventure, storms
and possibilities.
Eyes gazing at the natural world,
pools of admiration and
revelry in the magic of seasons and cycles.
His eyes, her eyes, their eyes all
sending out an invitation,
windows open to the perceptive seer.

My words found a place to land.

A free verse revealed.

Is it good? Does it matter?

Bad doesn't even exist,

besides it is mine, no value statements allowed.

Spontaneous words fall out on the page

and energize me.

I am exalted and transported to a place far

away from searching, from struggle.

I am exalted, a bit fearful, too, so many words I never knew,

an offertory to my poised pen,

temporarily living outside of the constraints of

the rational.

Trust the flow of words, running the rapids of

pure blissful freedom.

They come with the steady flow of the river

and the possibility that a drier time may come,

then trusting in the rains that will

fill the great reservoir again and again,

allowing me to remain

expansive, hopeful, waiting.

Inspiration, divine guidance,

an infinite landscape to choose from,

a breath that is eternally mine.

Each a healer, mind, body, and soul.
Each offering salient solace and support.
Each walking their talk and talking little,
listening poignantly.
Each poised to offer her life wisdom and
gifts of graceful words with neutral
and gentle power.

Each emerging as sojourners holding
the hope of
transformation,
tweaking my thoughts,
my habits and beliefs.
Each eager to see me discover
the mysteries within myself,
the rich soil of self-love and
unconditional acceptance.

Three women created a circle where I
flowed from outside the space
to inside the inner sanctuary of
the sphere of protection.
Held in love and support
for many days and years.
I flowed from outside to inside,
to eventually discover that I
was healed enough to join the
sacred circle of mighty women
offering hope and freedom to others.

I know truth when I see it.
Filling all the spaces inside with light,
a monochromatic palette transforming before me
into an inclusive riot of colors.
Pixel by pixel, falling softly before my
inner and outer eyes,
capturing beauty and holding it before me,
noticing all subtleties,
a message without doubt or fear.

I know truth when I hear it.
Resounding with waves of sincere amens,
spoken in whispers, gently and confidently,
falling syllable by syllable on my ears,
like wide open spaces of gentle winds carrying particles
of resonance and trust.

I know truth when I feel it,
Stepping into and through new doors,
always flung wide open, inviting me to come forth,
embracing what lies before me.
Standing on the shoulders of sages and enlightened ones,
its satin finish slides along my skin satisfying my need for
touch and the deep warmth of knowing.
Inhaling energy, exhaling belief.

She played the flat keys with
tentative and stretching fingers,
chords without sound,
melody without a rhythm for her ear,
counting the silent beats,
hoping the practice would
yield a deeper, richer tone when
she took her turn at the ebony, ivory
keys shared by all.
Now her practice,
the slow breaths of meditation,
counting the in and out,
avoiding the distractions, reaching
across and above the layers of thoughts
to the place of peaceful contentment,
not striving for a perfect melody,
yet listening for the silent sounds
and quiet mindfulness
suggesting
a temporary nirvana,
a concerto of
measurable breaths.

all our tomorrows new

Let's make new news, our world new,
not the same
reports and unreported cases
of violence and oppression.
Four hundred years of history.
we can't change it,
but we can make today and all
our tomorrows new.
Imagine living among
stories of hope, expressions of unity,
recorded moments of
color-based thinking thoroughly
and permanently abolished,
losing our fixed mindset and
seeing forever through a different lens.
Why has it taken so many so many casualties?
Why has it taken so much despair?
Why has it taken so many pasts and futures?
Why won't get us there. Only change will.

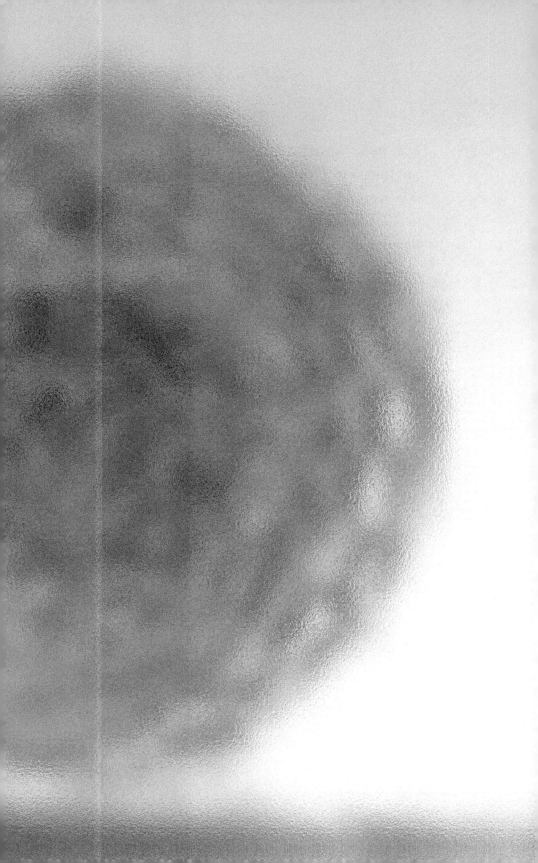

At the altar of the Divine Feminine I am healed,
recognizing my broken pieces are an illusion.
Holding in the love and light,
all mothers and grandmothers before me,
those who did not find the Divine Presence
of an earthly or divine mother,
who did not receive or offer unconditional love.

For mothers who found no reservoir of fullness,
compassion or creativity,
who lived with the awareness of missing parts,
striving to find an opening to something greater,
something to ease the cycle of indifference,
the avoidance of feelings and actions.
Each feeling broken, depleted by the
unattainable promise of wholeness.

In this moment,
mothers opening to
Divine Love and Wisdom,
whole and joyful,
abounding with the pure
healing power of the One.

Breaking generational cycles,
Softening deep wounds of
heart, body and soul.
A child, a daughter looking for acceptance,
worth, an open hand or open heart.
Never finding the pure solace of a warm embrace or
being seen through the pure,
unfiltered eyes of unconditional love,
joy in the sheer miracle of her existence.

In this moment a child healing
from indifference by loving others deeply,
letting love seep into every fiber of their being.
Finding Wholeness, their worthiness in their sheer existence,
their fullness in God's open embrace,
Divine Love and Perfection.
Breaking generational cycles,
healing deep wounds in heart, body and soul.

at the altar

Notorious they called her,
her infamy for the battles
she fought, for the unity
she nurtured,
breaking down walls to the
left and right.
Higher intelligence
was her justice.

Her notoriety, a reward for her
fearlessness, courage
and relentless spirit.
She lived her passion for law,
shattering ceilings that kept
citizens waiting for too many decades
to find the freedom they
deserved.

Opinions formed from the depth of
her soul, labors of her love for her
sisters and brothers.
Her convictions made her transcendent,
and we joined her army, following
our five-foot-one fearless leader through the
trenches, the halls, the chambers where

her words, spoken in humble tones,
challenged each to resist, to desist
and march with conviction to a better
day.

*Note: Written to commemorate Supreme Court Justice
Ruth Bader Ginsburg, known as Notorious RBG.

notorious

endless jewels

In my thoughts the world was small,
limited by trivial details of
what if, maybe it will, maybe it won't.
Vast reaches I cannot fathom as I try
to squeeze the infinite into a grain of sand,
forgetting the limitless boundaries
of its domain.
I stumble into moments of sadness,
where darkness threatens to engulf me,
then gratitude leads me back to the light,
light brilliant, I reach higher, surpassing
other moments of hope,
so I may remember that life is infinite,.

Intention unbridled, I create a mosaic of life.
My words, my thoughts and my actions
deliberate, conscious.
All that is possible from eons and eons,
back and forth, spill out like
endless jewels from the hand of the divine.
No limits, my breath says.
No limits, my heart beats.
No limits, I repeat.

trust and surrender

Trust and surrender,
written all over the pages of life,
a personal letting go.
Like trapeze artists reaching up and out,
for hands to meet mid-air.
I climb the stairs of the swinging ladder,
face the future with trust,
looking into the face of fear and doubt.
Knowing that I am one with life,
unwavering faith, the catalyst for this
ride I choose.
I fly, my connection destined by the
pure and simple act of surrender.
Caught and released to
float in the circle
of love and protection.
Each time a deeper union.
Each time an abundant yes!

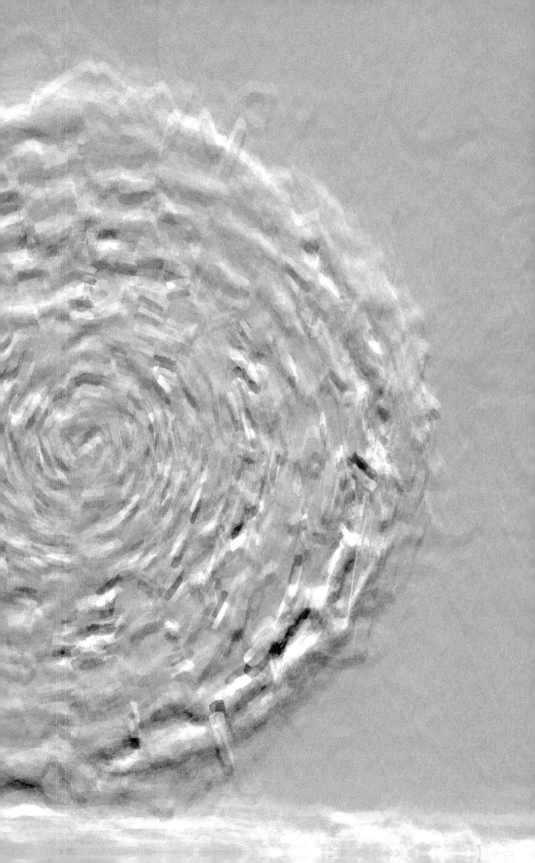

gardens

In Spring, I planted seeds,
sown seeds of change,
days and weeks followed
and secret confidences
were whispered,
quiet explosions in the earth's rich
humus.
A promise was hailed by the limitless
potential of each seed and a garden
was the piece of heaven I expected
to be revealed.
This time the seasonal rhythm of day and night
felt different, the promise I awaited
would give more than a fleeting
glimpse of color and smell, attention and pause.
I was waiting for hope, for resurrection.
In the right time,
the only time for
the fruition of our sowing to
demonstrate its form, my garden
heralded an effect beyond my
imagined scape.
Resurrected from ancient seeds,
generations of ancestral cycles of
birth offered a glimpse of possibility,
and greater too a beckoning call
to thrive in this new soil.

Absolute,
all there is and
all that I am,
here this moment,
and all moments
beyond eternity.
Unimaginable,
mystical proportions
of perfection,
vast and consummate,
enveloping, an embrace of
the peace of oneness.

Receptive
to the new each moment,
accepting our thoughts, the seeds
of change and action,
open heartedly spilling effects with
sheer, voluminous joy in giving,
listening to billions of sown
ruminations, tuning all to the
symphony of form and oneness.

Divine wisdom,
a sacred trust,

attuned and
one with the natural
world, all Life,
realization of the power
within and without,
the brilliant illumination
of the open heart.
Reality brushed with truth,
dappled with points of light,
fashioning a portrait of oneness.

Unlimited,
infinite and irrepressible,
orchestrating the planets
and stars,
each atom in perfect motion,
each form filling the
spaces of the
One Life,
One Presence.
I am absolute, receptive, divine wisdom,
unlimited.   Oneness.

qualities

Don't lose gratitude for the sun,
I reminded myself,
Just because the earth appears
scorched or flooded,
temperatures rise, icebergs melt,
forests become ash and we wonder
about the seasons
seeming to be stuck
in a fixed state of motion
around the sun.
Our faces still lift and tilt
toward this radiant orb of
promise and nurture.
Our homage is a perfect
symphony driven by the
sheer power of energy,
solar droplets of deep
desire.
Perched millions of miles
and light years away we
are silent partners,
all beacons of life on
our home.

In that room, that simple room,
souls united,
unfathomed possibilities
found grounding,
light and hope reborn
made the unfolding of the journey
an inspired quest for wholeness.
Reverent eyes, extended hands,
fertile silences, gentle
words wove a cocoon
around the two so that
destiny brought peace
and solidarity,
making what seemed impossible,
a healing wholeness.
That simple room,
rife with love and acceptance,
trust and purity,
set the course for an awakening,
indelible and divine.

love has never heard of hate

Love has never heard of hate,
is never burdened by fear
or insecurity, never stands face to face
or side by side with inequity,
never doubts its fullness,
its limitlessness.
Encircles its domain, extending
unconditional acceptance.

Love has never heard of hate,
powerful beyond all measure,
a philanthropist of abundance.
Creation echoes this generosity,
a mirror of the organic
openness resonating through
its masses.

Love has never heard of hate,
Never grappled with what belonged or
what was worthy, knows implicitly that
it holds all of us in its warm embrace.
Only a matter of time before we all
know which side we belong on.

sunshine bliss

My cat stretches out on the carpet before me in
pure sunshine bliss, the shiny spot is small,
yet she wiggles her body into
its warm embrace,
a circle of light meant for her alone.
I sit in the chair doing the same,
my sunshine bliss is a quiet moment of
union meant for all.
She releases, I expand.
I release, she deepens into peace.

We both open our hearts and sing different songs
to the same source.
Grateful for the space we create,
I watch her and revere her single mindedness.
She is in the moment, effortlessly embracing her union.
I inhale, committing to the moment second by second,
using breath to keep me here,
embracing the union I seek and find.
She dreams of nowhere else, nothing else in this holy time.
I watch and learn from her,
growing in my ease with the simple act
of being.

Open to the gentle tapping
of the bird at the window,
the fluttering wings of the butterfly,
the strata of orange, red and purple at sunset.
Remember the ancient secret, shouted from
the mountaintops,
find it brilliantly shining in
the constellations,
emerging from the
depths of the ocean and carried on the waves
to the shores of our personal and collective lives.

We are spiritual beings having a
human experience.
Born into this human form,
then too often, believing
we left the spiritual on the other side,
believing we will find it again on the other side.
Suffering and struggling to
make ourselves whole by
splitting ourselves into pieces,
commissioned to the
corners of our world
to find what,
we already have.

It's Christmas and I
hold an orange chapstick,
hand-knitted stockings and a
homemade card with crayon
circles, peace comes in
simple and small packages.
Amid the snowy mountains,
a frozen pond and star-studded skies,
peace comes to me in the soft, cold silence.
The aroma of burning piñon logs,
warm pine needles and
baked cookies
arrives on my inhale,
peace comes to me on the gentle stirrings.
Loved ones gathering, young and old
share my sense of family and
tears roll down my face, a stream
of salty droplets while
peace comes to me from
deep love and resonance.
Together we sing,
luminarias and farolitas
light the night,
a song created by
sweet notes, drifting up and

down the scales,
peace comes to
me from the convergence
of voices.
A satisfying embrace,
heartbeat to heartbeat
then the deep breaths sigh,
the sound of complete peace.
Savor these moments,
each offering awareness,
a graceful dab of
gratitude for the oneness
that we are.

peace

Say yes,
when harvest seems plentiful,
and gratitude fills all the spaces.
Say yes,
when divine love encircles us,
a warm embrace of hope and home,
when the path is laid clear before us..

Say yes,
when contraction pulls you in,
when all the power in the
universe seems powerless to
shape your thoughts,
to sow under
false thoughts that blind you.

Say yes,
when the power of
all the oceans
ebb and flow to empower you
to see possibilities with
majestic clarity.

Say yes,
when rising above daily challenges

rests on the slightest adjustment
of attention and action.

Say yes,
when our light
seems to have dimmed,
when thoughts lean into
can't and shouldn't,
Say yes,
when why sends us on
a spiraling path we rather
avoid, feeling
limit and doubt.

Say yes because you can,
hope is renewable.
Say yes because
you know how to walk the tightrope of light
in a world where there is only
good and hard is just a temporary
challenge that can't make you stick
to a state of mind that refuses to
see its own resilience.

say yes!

the artist

How far will I go to
resist the inertia that
drags me closer to the earth
and farther from the stars,
closer to the finite and farther
from the infinite?

I have the power to change
my worldview,
to view the world
from heart, not head,
to stop thinking so much
about mistakes and blunders
painted in the pictures
I see when the media shows
me a world I wouldn't shape.

My automatic worldview
can forget that
choices matter,
each thought,
each feeling,

each action creates
an effect,
a perspective I
want to believe.

I am the artist who
paints pictures of
hope and change,
the author writing prose
and poetry to ignite
love and wisdom.
How limitless is infinite,
How immeasurable is goodness?
So many paintings and stories
waiting to be revealed.

the artist

Each breath, each step,
clearly aligned with an unconditional
state of mind,
consciously deepening each thought,
each feeling and action
with truth.
Not fleeting desires,
sustainable, a fidelity incomprehensible
as all the grains of sand and stars in the sky.
Love myself first, recognize who I am
and always have been,
essential and renewable,
perfect in intention.
Being Love, faith defeating fear.
Microcosm and macrocosm have no limits.
Boundless, once and for all.

falling forward

I walk by falling forward,
a trust fall into
the arms of Life.
I move forward, new steps
each new moment.
I fall forward, aligned, receptive,
joyful with each step.
Falling in love, embracing the
perfect patterns of the Divine
Presence.
I walk, I run,
arms wide open,
I twirl through spaces once
filled with discord and fear.
Reality shifts as I move,
emboldened by a deep sense
of Oneness and Power.
Movement with eyes and mind
wide open, expanses before me,
I see present and
future as limitless,
calling me to complete
abandon again and again.

Note: "We walk by falling forward...."
Ernest Holmes,
The Essential Ernest Holmes, *p.33*

the light around us

I climbed the kiva ladder
rung by rung, year after year,
emerging one day into the light,
on what seemed to be
the apex of my journey,
yet turned out to be one of many
more awakenings.
We are new every minute,
infinite possibilities
for going beyond each
perceived apex
into greater and greater light.
Everywhere it shines,
in all things it shines,
Before each step it shines,
Calling us to Life, to be the light.

affirmation for oneness

I am the rain,
falling gently,
nourishing the land
that I am.

I am the sky, blue and bright
palette for the soaring birds
that I am.

I am the ocean, cleansing bath for
the seals and seagulls
that I am.

I am the mountains,
strong monuments
to the powerful presence
of the divine
that I am.

I am the gnarly, outstretched branches
of the venerable oak tree welcoming
thousands of species of invertebrates
that I am.

All Life, I AM.

She was small and
I couldn't see how she could help me
until she became so big that her
superpowers threw a web around
my despair and gave me a place to
land over and over again.
Her voice echoed mantras for my
reprogramming, words of encouragement
and unconditional acceptance,
words to help me believe in my worthiness.
Sound became a heartbeat that pushed
the blood back into my veins,
allowing me to choose to thrive
rather than survive.

Her eyes oceanic invited me
to swim in the deep waters of
compassion and trust,
pulling me out with their ebb,
out to sea for the replenishment
of my wholeness and
bringing me back into my life fuller,
nourished with each flow.
Her hands, a nest for protection from
the things I didn't want to remember.

Hands pulsating with fidelity gently reconciled
me to my many parts.
Learning a new language,
a new rhythm of breathing.

There is a light at the end of the tunnel
she said for many, many years,
then miraculously I stood in the light and
proclaimed it for myself.
Mutually hopeful, trusting the path
for thousands of days
or thousands of years,
we walked step by step and
word by word,
till we met ourselves radiant.

radiant

word by word

I heard it word by word,
but no pen or paper handy,
I worried all the way home that
I wouldn't remember
the words that sounded perfect and
wrote themselves through the air,
carried on the wind and the wings of inspiration.
An inner voice proclaimed that they were mine
if I could just catch them.
The poet's words delivered on the wind
and warmed by the sun,
grace from somewhere outside of myself,
transformed by my hands from wind to paper,
surely something bigger than me.
Where does inspiration live?
What does she look like?
If I could see her coming or knew
when she would deliver the poem,
the short story, the path to a piece
of artwork, I could be better
prepared.
On a long walk in the early light of morning,
catching a few extra sleepy moments,
bathing in a pool of warm, effervescent water,
talking on the phone or watching a movie.

It comes out of nowhere,
or out of somewhere so magnificent,
a "place" so eloquent with words and images,
so full of richness and melody,
dropping the lines or the images one at a time.
I step aside, I bow to the divine intervention,
awakening from my slumberous state
of being in the middle time,
between works of rhyme or fiction, images and ideas.
I will be ready next time or I will catch only
what I can from the fleeting, pulsating,
pure sweet light of the gift that seeks me.

word by word

about the author

janice ballard

Janice Ballard has lived in Santa Fe, New Mexico, for more than thirty years. The Southwest, with its wide-open spaces, mountain views, and wildlife, appeals to her sense of home. This is her first published volume of poetry.

10&36

Made in the USA
Monee, IL
07 October 2021